HOLIDAY DESSERTS

BARBOUR
PUBLISHING, INC.
Uhrichsville, Ohio

© MCMXCVII by Barbour Publishing, Inc.

ISBN 1-57748-110-0

All rights reserved. No part of this publication may be reproduced or transmitted in any form or by any means without written permission of the publisher.

Published by Barbour Publishing, Inc.
P.O. Box 719
Uhrichsville, Ohio 44683
http://www.barbourbooks.com

Printed in the United States of America.

My Easiest and Best Dessert

Grease 8x13-inch pan

Place in bottom:
2 cups apple sauce
1 20-oz. can crushed pineapple

Sprinkle over the above:
1 pkg. dry white cake mix

Dribble over the above:
1 cup melted butter

Sprinkle over the above:
1/2 cup chopped nuts

Bake at 350°F for 30 minutes.

Delores Hernerding—Duluth, MN

APPLE-BLUEBERRY CRISP

2 1/2 cups sliced, peeled apples
1 cup blueberries, fresh or frozen
1/2 cup granulated sugar
1 T. flour
1/2 tsp. cinnamon
1/4 tsp. salt
3/4 cup oatmeal (regular or quick)
3/4 cup flour
3/4 cup brown sugar
1/4 tsp. baking powder
1/4 tsp. baking soda
1/4 tsp. cinnamon
1/3 cup melted butter

Place apple slices in a buttered 9x9-inch pan or pie plate. Mix granulated sugar, 1 T. flour, cinnamon, and salt together. Sprinkle evenly over apples and blueberries. Combine oatmeal, 3/4 cup flour, brown sugar, soda, baking powder, 1/4 tsp. cinnamon, and butter. Mix until crumbly and sprinkle over apples and berries. Bake at 350°F for 30-40 minutes until bubbly and lightly browned. Serve warm with cream or ice cream.

Karen Brouillette—Hazen, ND

SCRIPTURE BREAD

2 1/2 cups flour	2 Samuel 13:8
5 tsp. baking powder	Galatians 5:9
1/2 tsp. salt	Mark 9:50
3/4 tsp. cinnamon	1 Kings 10:10
3 T. butter	Proverbs 30:33
3/4 cup sugar	Jeremiah 6:20
1 egg	Isaiah 10:14
3/4 cup milk	1 Corinthians 3:2
1 1/2 cups apples	Proverbs 25:11
1/2 cup raisins	1 Samuel 30:12

Follow Numbers 11:8. Preheat oven to 350°F Pare, core, and dice apples. Sift dry ingredients together. Cream butter and sugar. Add egg to butter mixture and mix well. Add dry ingredients, alternately with milk. Mix in apples and raisins gently. Pour into greased loaf pan. Bake approximately 90 minutes. Allow to cool.

Charlotte Setter—Dewey, AZ

RHUBARB BUTTER CRUNCH

4-5 cups rhubarb
Put in bottom of 9x13-inch pan

Mix together 1 cup sugar and 3 T. flour (if frozen rhubarb is used, add an extra T. of flour). Sprinkle this on top of rhubarb.

Mix the following together:
1 cup brown sugar
1 cup oatmeal
1 1/2 cups flour

Then add:
1/2 cup butter-flavored shortening
1/2 cup shortening

Use a pastry cutter tool to mix the two shortenings into the brown sugar, oatmeal, and flour mixture. Then sprinkle this on top of rhubarb.

Bake at 375°F for 40 minutes.

Rose Wruck—Hazen, ND

PUMPKIN CRISP

1 large can pumpkin
1 large can evaporated milk
3 eggs
1 cup sugar
1/2 tsp. cinnamon
1 cup chopped nuts
1 box yellow cake mix
2 sticks margarine, melted and cooled

Grease and flour 9x13-inch pan. Mix pumpkin, milk, sugar, eggs, and cinnamon and put in pan. Pour dry cake mix over. Put nuts into mix evenly. Spoon melted and cooled margarine over mix. Bake at 350°F for 50 to

60 minutes. Top with whipped cream when serving.

Debbie Lovett—Dubuque, IA

BAKED APPLES IN CARAMEL CREAM

3 T. brown sugar
1/4 cup hot water
Combine in 8-inch baking dish
4 large apples (cored)
1 T. lemon juice
12 caramels
1/2 cup whipping cream

Peel top half of apple, brush with lemon juice. Fill each apple with 3 caramels. Bake at 350°F for 65 minutes. Baste with syrup every 20 minutes. Place apples in individual dishes. Pour remaining sauce into pan; add cream. Cook mixture until smooth and pour over apples.

Tracy Bentley-Runge—Ft. Thomas, KY

Laura's Dessert Delight

1/2 cup margarine
1 cup flour
1/2 cup finely chopped pecans

1 8-oz. pkg. cream cheese
1 cup whipped topping (divided)
1 cup powdered sugar
Shredded coconut (optional)

1 cup milk
1 pkg. instant chocolate pudding
1 cup milk
1 pkg. instant vanilla pudding
Toasted pecan pieces

Heat oven to 350°F. Lightly grease 9x13-inch pan. Mix margarine, flour, and pecans. Press into bottom of baking pan. Bake 15-20 minutes until light brown. Cool.

Mix cream cheese, cool whip, powdered sugar. Spread over cooled crust.

Optional: Sprinkle with coconut to cover.

Beat chocolate pudding and milk. Pour over cream cheese layer. Beat vanilla pudding and milk. Pour over the chocolate layer. Cover with the remaining whipped topping and sprinkle with coconut and pecans. Keep refrigerated.

Options: sliced bananas, strawberries, different flavors of puddings.

Jenny Resendez—Port Arthur, TX

DAD'S CHRISTMAS AMBROSIA

1 fresh coconut
8 bananas
8 oranges
Sugar—enough to cover each layer.

Crack the coconut. Scrape the meat from the shell. Flake it. Use a large crock and make a layer of each—bananas, oranges, and coconut. Sprinkle lightly with sugar. Continue until ingredients are used up. Let stand over night.

Laura Jansen—Battle Creek, MI

COCONUT CRUNCH DESSERT
Yield: 12-16 servings

1/2 cup butter or margarine, melted
1 cup all-purpose flour
1 1/4 cups flaked coconut
1/4 cup packed brown sugar
1 cup slivered almonds
1 pkg. (3.4 oz.) instant vanilla pudding mix.
1 pkg. (3.4 oz.) instant coconut pudding mix
2 2/3 cups cold milk
2 cups whipped topping

Combine the first five ingredients; press lightly into a greased 13x9x2-inch baking pan. Bake at 350°F for 25-30 minutes or until a golden brown, stirring every 10 minutes to form coarse crumbs. Cool. Divide crumb mixture in half; press half into the same baking pan. In a mixing bowl, beat pudding mixes and milk. Fold in whipped topping; spoon over the crust. Top with remaining crumb mixture. Cover and refrigerate overnight.

Joanne Moyer—Johnson City, TN

Four Layer Dessert

1 cup flour
1/2 cup butter or margarine, softened
1 cup chopped walnuts
1 8-oz. pkg. cream cheese, softened
1 cup powdered sugar
1 12-oz. container whipped topping, divided
2 small pkgs. instant pudding (any flavor)
3 cups cold milk
Additional chopped nuts or chocolate curls

For crust, mix together flour, butter, and chopped nuts. Press into 9x13-inch pan and bake 15 minutes at 350°F or until golden brown. Cool. In mixing bowl, beat cream cheese and powdered sugar until smooth; stir in 1 cup whipped topping. Spread over cooled crust. Add cold milk to pudding mix and beat until slightly thickened. Pour over cream cheese layer. Top with remaining whipped topping and sprinkle additional nuts on top if desired. May use chocolate curls if using chocolate pudding. Chill at least 4 hours.

Jayne Pokorny—Ewing, NE

STRAWBERRY ANGEL CREAM DESSERT

1 prepared Angel Food cake
1 14-oz. cup sweetened condensed milk
1 cup cold water
1 tsp. vanilla
1 small pkg. instant vanilla pudding
1 pt. whipping cream
2 21-oz. cans strawberry pie filling

Cut cake into 1/4-inch slices and arrange 1/2 of the cake into a 9x13-inch pan. In mixing bowl, combine milk, water, vanilla, and pudding. Mix well. Chill for 10 minutes. Fold in whipped cream. Spread 1/2 of this mixture over the cake. Top with 1 can of strawberries. Repeat. Chill 4 hours before serving.

Pam Goudzward—Oak Forest, IL

APPLE BUTTERSCOTCH CAKE

1 cup shortening
3 eggs
2 cups sugar
3 cups self-rising flour
3 cups sliced apples
6 oz. butterscotch morsels
2 tsp. vanilla
1 1/2 cups chopped nuts

Mix oil, eggs, and sugar until creamed. Add flour and vanilla. Add remaining ingredients. Bake 1 hour at 350°F in tube or loaf pans.

Wanda Johnson—Monroeville, AL

BAKLAVA

2 lb. filo dough
2 cups walnuts
1 lb. sweet butter, melted
Ground clove
1/2 cup sugar
Cinnamon

Syrup:
2 cups water
2 cups sugar
1/2 cup honey

Grind nuts and add 1/2 cup of sugar. Add cinnamon and ground clove, to your taste. Mix well. Brush a 12x16x2-inch baking tray with melted butter. Place 3-5 pieces of strudel leaves at bottom of pan and pour some melted butter over the entire sheet. Repeat until 1 lb. of filo is used. Spread chopped walnuts evenly. Repeat above directions with second package of filo. Baste the top leaves well with melted butter. With pointed knife, score top sheets in diamond or square shapes. Bake at 350°F for

1 hour, then increase heat until top becomes golden brown. Combine ingredients for syrup and heat through. Pour hot syrup over cooled baklava (or pour cold syrup over hot baklava).

Lauren McMann, Blairsville, GA

CHERRY HOLIDAY CAKE
Yield: 24-30 servings

1 pkg. white cake mix
2 8-oz. cream cheese
4 cups confectioners sugar
1 pt. whipping cream
2 21-oz. cherry pie filling

Prepare cake according to package directions. Pour into two greased 13x9x2-inch cake pans or a jelly-roll pan. Bake at 350°F for 20 minutes or until toothpick comes out clean. Cool. In mixing bowl, beat the cream cheese and sugar until fluffy in separate bowl. Beat the whipping cream until firm;

fold into cream cheese mixture. Spread over cake. Top with pie filling. Chill 4 hours or overnight.

Stephanie Mayer—Bellevue, NE

FAN HUNTER'S CUSTARD

1 gallon whole milk
1 dozen egg yolks
1 cup sugar
1 T. cornstarch
1-2 T. vanilla extract
Whipped Cream
Maraschino cherries
Ice cream (optional)

Heat milk in a double boiler. Beat egg yolks, sugar, and cornstarch (with a little milk to prevent lumps). Add to heated milk. Cook until it feels thick (coats a metal spoon). Chill overnight. Before serving, stir in vanilla. Serve in tall sherbet glasses, topped with a mound of whipped cream. Place a maraschino cherry on top and eat with a small spoon. It can also be served over a scoop of ice cream.

Elaine Howard—Elsberry, MO

BANANA SPLIT CAKE

2 cups graham cracker crumbs
1 stick margarine, melted.
Mix and put in bottom of 9x13-inch pan. Chill.

2 sticks margarine
2 cups powdered sugar
2 eggs
1 tsp. vanilla
Beat no less than 15 minutes or until mixture turns creamy white in color. Spread on top of graham cracker crust.

Add layers in order given:
1 can crushed pineapple, drained; 4 or 5

bananas sliced; 1 9-oz. container whipped topping; chopped nuts; maraschino cherries. Spread evenly on top.

Keep refrigerated.

Cherie Hein—Richardson, TX

PEACHES-N-CREAM CHEESECAKE

3/4 cup flour
1 3-oz. pkg. vanilla pudding
3 T. margarine
1 tsp. baking powder
1/2 tsp. salt
1 egg
1/2 cup milk

Beat together and put in bottom of 9x9-inch pan. Put sliced peaches on top.

Mix:
8 oz. cream cheese

1/2 cup sugar
3 T. peach juice
Pour over peaches.

Mix:
1 T. sugar
1/2 tsp. cinnamon
Sprinkle over top.

Bake 350°F for 30-35 minutes or until crust is golden brown.

Julianne Troyer—Conneauville, PA

DANISH BRAIDS
Yield: 4 braids

5 cups flour
1/2 tsp. salt
1 cup butter (room temperature)
3 eggs
1 pkg. active dry yeast
1/4 cup warm water
3/4 cup warm water

1/2 cup sugar

Filling:
1 cup butter, softened
1 cup brown sugar
1 T. cinnamon
1 cup chopped pecans

Glaze:
1 1/2 cups powdered sugar
1-2 T. hot milk
3 tsp. butter, melted
1/2 tsp. vanilla

Cut butter in flour and salt in large mixing bowl with pastry cutter until mixture is flaky. Dissolve yeast in 1/4 cup warm water. Add eggs, yeast mixture, 3/4 cup water, and sugar to flour mixture. Mix until dough is well mixed (batter may be sticky). Refrigerate, covered, for 5 to 6 hours or overnight. Bring dough to room temperature, about 1 hour. Divide dough into 4 equal parts. Roll each part into a 12x9-inch rectangle (like a thin cinnamon roll) on floured surface.

Prepare filling by combining ingredients until well mixed. Using 1/2 cup filling per braid, spread a 3 inch wide strip down the center of each rectangle. With kitchen shears (or knife), cut sides toward center in strips, 3 inches long and 1 inch wide. Fold strips over filling, alternating from side to side. Place on greased cookie sheet. Cover and let rise until double the size, about 1 hour. Bake at 350°F for 20 to 25 minutes. Carefully remove to wire rack. Cool slightly. Mix glaze ingredients until smooth. Dribble glaze on top of braids. Braids freeze well.

Glenna Carroll—Golden, OK

FUNNEL CAKES

1 1/3 cups flour
1 1/4 tsp. salt
1/2 tsp. soda
2 T. sugar
3/4 T. baking powder

Sift together above ingredients in a bowl.

1 egg
3/4 cup milk

Mix egg and milk together. Add to dry ingredients. Beat until smooth. Heat some oil in wok or skillet.

Using either a funnel or squeeze bottle (old pancake syrup bottle works well), pour batter into oil. Us a circular motion starting from the inside and work your way outside in a tight spiral. Cook 1 to 2 minutes on one side and turn with tongs. Cook additional minute until brown and crispy. Remove onto paper towels and sprinkle with cinnamon-sugar or powdered sugar. Eat immediately!

Charlotte Shopmeyer—Evansville, IN

CHOCOLATE EATERS CAKE

1 pkg. 18.5-oz. chocolate cake mix
1 pkg. 3 3/4-oz. vanilla instant pudding
1 pkg. 3 3/4-oz. chocolate instant pudding
4 eggs

1 cup cooking oil
1 cup buttermilk
1 cup chocolate chips
1 cup black walnuts

Combine all ingredients. Beat at medium speed 4 minutes. Stir in 1 cup black walnuts, 1 cup chocolate chips. Mix well. Pour in 12-cup bundt pan. Bake at 350°F 50 minutes. Turn out on serving place. Sprinkle with powdered sugar. (Can be baked a day early.)

Dorothy L. Schultz—Theodosia, MO

FRESH APPLE CAKE

4 cups apples, peeled and cut up
2 cups sugar
2 cups flour
2 tsp. baking soda
1 tsp. salt
2 tsp. cinnamon

1/2 cup oil
2 eggs, beaten
2 tsp. vanilla
1 cup chopped nuts

Sprinkle sugar over apples. Sift dry ingredients; mix well with apples. Stir in oil, eggs, and vanilla. Add nuts. Pour in oiled and floured fluted bundt pan. Bake 50 minutes at 375°F. Cool 15 minutes and invert.

Joyce Lee—Cola, SC

PEARLY GATE CAKE

1 cup shortening
3 cups sugar
5 cups flour
4 tsp. baking powder
1/2 tsp. salt
2 cups water
8 egg whites (beaten)
1 tsp. lemon extract

1/2 tsp. almond extract

Blend shortening and sugar with a mixer. Sift flour, baking powder, and salt 3 times. Now alternately add flour mixture and water (2 T. at time) to sugar mixture. Add 1/2 of the egg whites; continue putting in flour and water until it's all gone. Now add remaining egg whites and extracts. Mix; then pour into three 9-inch layer pans. Bake at 325°F for 25 to 30 minutes. Let cool, then frost with white icing. Serve.

April Gandy—Russellville, AL

NEW ORLEANS PRALINE CHEESECAKE

1 1/2 cups graham cracker crumbs
3 T. sugar
3 T. melted butter or margarine
3 8-oz. pkg. cream cheese
3/4 cup firmly packed brown sugar
2 T. all-purpose flour

3 eggs
2 tsp. vanilla extract
1/2 cup finely chopped pecans
Whipping cream and pecan halves

Combine first 3 ingredients. Mix well. Press mixture into a 9-inch spring form pan. Bake at 350°F for 10 minutes. Beat cream cheese until smooth. Gradually add brown sugar and flour, mixing well. Add eggs, one at a time, beating well after each. Stir in vanilla and chopped pecans. Pour into prepared pan. Bake for 40 to 45 minutes. Let cool to room temperature on rack. Refrigerate overnight. Remove sides of spring form pan, top cheese cake with whipped cream or whipped topping. Garnish with pecan halves.

Lorraine Pierce—Cut Off, LA

CREAM CHEESE POUND CAKE

1 cup margarine, softened
1/2 cup butter, softened
1 8-oz. pkg. cream cheese, softened
3 cups sugar
6 eggs
3 cups sifted cake flour
2 tsp. vanilla extract

Combine first 3 ingredients; beat well with heavy duty mixer. Gradually add sugar; beat well until light and fluffy. Add eggs, one at a time; beat well after each addition. Add flour to creamed mixture; beat well. Stir in vanilla. Pour batter into a greased and floured 10 inch tube pan. Bake at 325°F for 1 hour and 30 minutes. Cool in pan 15 minutes. Remove from pan and cool completely.

Earnestine Jackson—Beaumont, TX

Million Dollar Pound Cake

3 cups sugar
1 pound butter (4 sticks), softened
6 eggs (room temperature)
4 cups all-purpose flour
3/4 cup milk
1/2 tsp. almond extract
1 1/2 tsp. vanilla extract

Combine sugar and butter; cream until light and fluffy. Add eggs, one at a time, beating well after each addition. Add flour to mixture one cup at a time, alternating with milk, beating well after each addition. Stir in extracts. Pour batter into well-greased and floured (or sugared) tube pan. Bake at 300°F for 1 hour and 40 minutes. It will have a crusty top.

Lou Ann Allen—Alpine, AL

Emma's Christmas Bread

8 cups flour
2 cups milk
1 tsp. salt
2 pkgs. yeast
1 cup sugar
4 eggs
1 pound butter
2 cups candied fruit
1 cup seedless raisins
1/2 pound nuts
Grated rind of 1 lemon
1 tsp. ground cardamon

Set yeast with milk and stir in 1 cup flour. Let rise. Cream butter with sugar. Add eggs, beat well. Add lemon rind. Combine 3 mixtures, add flour, cardamon. Sprinkle 1 cup flour over the chopped fruit and nuts. Mix and add to dough, knead until smooth and elastic—about 10 minutes. Let rise double. Make into loaves and put in greased pans. Let rise. Bake 45 minutes in a preheated oven at 350°F.

Rosemary Hyman—Hawkeye, IA

BLENDER COCONUT CUSTARD PIE

2 cups milk
4 eggs
1/3 cup margarine
1/2 cup flour
3/4 cup sugar
1 cup coconut
1 1/2 tsp. vanilla
Dash nutmeg

In blender, combine all ingredients. Blend 1 minute. Pour into greased, floured 10-inch pie pan. Bake at 350°F for 1 hour or until golden brown.

Mimi Galsterer—Garo, MI

Pumpkin Pie

1 unbaked pie shell—8 or 9-inch
1 cup cooked pumpkin
3/4 cup sugar
2 T. flour
2 eggs
3/4 cup milk
1/2 tsp. cinnamon
1/2 tsp. ginger
1/2 tsp. nutmeg
1/2 tsp. salt

Mix all together. Strain into pie shell. If you want a thicker filling, use the 8-inch pie shell, building up the edges. Bake 425°F for 15 minutes. Reduce to 400°F. Bake until knife inserted an inch from the edge comes out clean. Center sets later.

Irene Hafermann—Edem, WI

Mama's Butterscotch Pie
Makes 8-inch pie.

1 cup light brown sugar
3 egg yolks
2 1/2 cups milk
3 1/2 to 4 T. flour (as needed to thicken)
2 T. vanilla
1 T. butter

Boil until thickened, stirring constantly.

Meringue:
3 egg whites
1/2 cup sugar
1/2 tsp. cream of tartar

Beat until frothy and stiff. Slowly add sugar and cream of tartar. Put on cooled pie. Bake at 325°F until tips are brown.

Linda Christian—Kenilworth, NJ

EASY PEANUT BUTTER PIE

1 graham cracker crust
1/2 cup crunchy peanut butter
3/4 cup powdered sugar
6 oz. cream cheese, softened
2 T. milk
8 oz. whipped topping

Cream the cream cheese and sugar together with mixer. Add peanut butter, milk and topping. Stir well. Pour into pie crust and chill 4-6 hours. Before serving, spread top with whipped topping or use dollops of whipped topping.

Ann Smithson—Starkville, MS

PEACHY PEACH COBBLER

2 cups of peaches
1/2 cup margarine (1 stick)
1 3/4 cups sugar

1 cup of flour
1 cup of milk

Combine peaches and 3/4 cups of sugar. Let stand for twenty minutes. Melt margarine in 1 1/2 quart baking dish. Mix flour and sugar. Add milk and mix. It will be lumpy. Pour into baking dish with peaches. Bake at 350°F for 45 minutes.

Dorothy Burford—Dalton, GA

MOUNTAIN HIGH BERRY PIE

2 egg whites
10 oz. frozen raspberries
1 cup sugar
1 T. lemon juice
1 cup whipped cream
9-inch pie shell

Beat egg whites. Add berries, sugar, lemon.

Beat 15 minutes—fold in whipped cream. Pour in pie shell and freeze overnight.

Nancy Schwartz—Normal, IL

SUGARLESS APPLE PIE

1 6-oz. can frozen apple juice concentrate
2 tsp. cinnamon
Dash of nutmeg
1/4 tsp. salt, optional
1 T. cornstarch
6 golden delicious apples, peeled and sliced.

Heat and stir the first five ingredients over medium heat until thick. Peel and slice 6 golden delicious apples. Mix together. Then pour into prepared pie crust. Cook 50 minutes in a preheated 425°F oven.

Pam Goudzwaard—Oak Forest, IL

Pecan Pie

3 eggs, beaten
1 cup dark corn syrup
1 cup brown sugar
2 T. melted butter
1 tsp. vanilla
2 cups pecans, broken
1 9-inch pie shell

Preheat oven to 350°F. Mix first five ingredients. Then add pecans. Mix well. Pour into crust. Bake 50 to 55 minutes or until knife inserted into center comes out clean. Delicious served with vanilla ice cream; or with a touch of maple syrup.

Sue Anderson—Jackman, ME

Chocolate Pie

Grandma's Pie Crust

1 cup unsifted flour
1/3 cup whipped butter
1/2 cup ice water

Combine 1 cup unsifted flour with a pinch of salt. Cut in 1/3 cup whipped butter. Add and stir with fork about 1/2 cup ice water until mixture holds together.

Form into ball, flour and roll out. Put in pie plate, flute edges and prick with fork. Bake at 375°F until brown on edges.

Chocolate Pie Filling

Mix:
3/4 cup sugar
3 T. cocoa
Dash salt
4 T. cornstarch

Scald 2 cups milk and add enough to make thin paste to above mixture. Add 3 beaten egg yolks. Then put this back into pan with rest of milk. Stir over medium heat until thick (approx. 7-10 minutes—if lumpy, stir with spoon until smooth). Remove from heat and stir in: 2 T. butter, 1 1/2 tsp. vanilla. Pour into prepared pie crust. Can top with meringue.

Sue Stovall—Dallas, TX

SWEDISH APPLE PIE

5-6 medium apples
   (Jonathan and Golden Delicious are
   good together)
1 T. sugar
1 T. cinnamon
3/4 cup melted butter (not margarine)
1 cup sugar
1 cup flour
1 egg
1/2 cup chopped nuts
Pinch of salt
Sprinkle of vanilla

Core and slice apples. Fill a 9 or 10-inch pie place 2/3 full with apples. Sprinkle sugar and cinnamon on top. Combine remaining ingredients. Pour over apples. Bake at 350°F for 45 minutes. (Easy to make—can top finished pie with whipped cream.)

Jackie Jeffries—Pottstown, PA

PINEAPPLE PIE

1 9-inch cookie crust or
    graham cracker crust
8 oz. cream cheese, softened
1 can sweetened condensed milk
1 20-oz. can crushed pineapple, drained
1/3 cup lemon juice
1 cup sour cream

Mix all ingredients and pour into shell. Refrigerate 3 hours. Can put whipped cream on top.

Beverly Neumann—Hilliard, OH

BLUEBERRY BUCKLE
Yield: 6 to 8 servings

1/4 cup margarine
3/4 cup sugar
1 egg
1/2 cup milk
2 cups flour
2 tsp. baking powder
1/2 tsp. salt
2 cups frozen blueberries
1/2 cup sugar
1/3 cup flour
1/4 cup margarine
1 tsp. cinnamon
1 tsp. grated lemon peel
1 tsp. grated orange peel

Cream margarine and sugar. Add egg and milk. Sift together dry ingredients and mix into creamed mixture. Mix well; fold blueberries gently into batter with a spoon. Pour batter into greased and floured 9-inch square pan. For topping, mix sugar, flour, margarine, cinnamon, and citrus peels until crumbly. Crumble on top of batter. Bake at 375°F for 35 to 45 minutes.

Elaine Clark—Wellington, KS

WOODFORD PUDDING

1 cup of sugar
1/2 cup butter
3 eggs
1 cup blackberry jam
1/2 cup flour
3 tsp. buttermilk
1 tsp. soda
1 tsp. cinnamon
1/2 tsp. nutmeg

Cream sugar and butter together. Add eggs and beat well. Add 1 cup of blackberry jam; stir in 1/2 cup flour. Mix buttermilk and soda together in separate bowl. Add buttermilk/soda combination, cinnamon and nutmeg, mix well. Bake at 350°F for 45 minutes or until firm. This will not be liquid pudding, but more like a bread-type pudding. Serve with sauce.

HARD SAUCE

1 cup butter
1 1/3 cups sugar
1 whole egg
1 cup half-and-half (or cream)

Mix well and cook in double boiler until thick. Flavor with 1 tsp. vanilla.

Kellane Hess—Ackworth, GA

JULE KAGA

2 cups milk, scalded
1/2 cup butter
1/3 cup warm water
1 pkg. dry yeast
1 T. sugar
2 1/2 cups flour
3/4 cup sugar

2 eggs, slightly beaten
1 1/2 cups raisins
1/4 cup citron (optional)
1 tsp. salt
1 tsp. ground cardamon
5 cups flour

Preheat oven to 350°F. Begin by scalding the milk and melting the butter in it. In separate bowl, dissolve water, yeast, and 1 T. sugar. Add all of these ingredients to the flour to make a soft dough. Cover and let rise until it bubbles. Add remaining ingredients. Add one cup of the flour in at a time, kneading until smooth. Cover and let rise in greased bowl until doubled in size. Then divide into 3 equal pieces. Put each piece in a round cake pan, greased. Cover. Let rise again about 1 hour. Bake at 350°F for 50 minutes. Best served warm or toasted.

Carol Giovanetto—Murdo, SD

Easy Rice Pudding

2 cups uncooked rice
1 can condensed milk
1 can golden raisins
1 tsp. vanilla
1/2 tsp. fresh nutmeg

Cook rice according to directions. Mix with condensed milk, raisins, and vanilla. Top with fresh nutmeg. Refrigerate.

Elaine Hull—Peachtree City, GA

Marshmallow Pudding

1 envelope Knox unflavored gelatin
1 cup hot water
1 cup sugar
1/2 tsp. vanilla
4 egg whites
1 cup nuts, finely chopped

Dissolve water and gelatin, and heat through.

Cool but do not let chill and begin to set. Beat egg whites very lightly, and add gelatin, then sugar, beating constantly. Divide into two parts. Add pink food coloring to one part of mixture, to shade desired. Add vanilla. Layer into glass bowl, separating the layers with ground or finely chopped dry-roasted peanuts. Other peanuts can be substituted.

Sharon Miller—Holmesville, OH

PUMPKIN CAKE ROLL

3 eggs
1 cup sugar
2/3 cup pumpkin
1 tsp. lemon juice
3/4 cup flour
1 tsp. baking powder
2 tsp. cinnamon
1 tsp. ginger
1/2 tsp. nutmeg
1/2 tsp. salt

1 cup nuts, chopped finely
Powdered sugar

Beat eggs at high speed for 5 minutes. Gradually beat in sugar. Stir in pumpkins and lemon juice. In a small bowl, sift together flour, baking powder, ginger, nutmeg, cinnamon, and salt. Fold into pumpkin mixture. Spread on well-greased 15x10x1-inch jelly roll pan. Top with 1 cup finely chopped nuts. Bake at 375°F for 15 minutes. Turn over onto a towel sprinkled with powdered sugar. Starting at narrow end, roll towel and cake together; cool. Unroll and spread filling on it.

Filling:
1 cup powdered sugar
6 oz. cream cheese, softened
4 T. butter
1 tsp. vanilla

Cream ingredients together and spread on cake; roll up. Serve.

Ruth Moyer—Bechtelsville, PA

FRUIT CAKE

1/2 cup butter
1 cup sugar
2 cups flour
2 eggs
1 tsp. baking soda
1 cup sour cream

Cream butter. Add sugar, flour, eggs, baking soda, and then sour cream.

Rind of 1 orange
1 cup of each: raisins, dates, and nuts
Pinch of salt

Grind these ingredients together. Combine with butter mixture. Bake at 350°F for 50 minutes.

Icing:
3/4 cup sugar
Juice of 1 orange

Pour icing over cake while hot.

Walli Mayer—Chicago Heights, IL